MANY PLACES TO SAVE ONE LIFE

Liam Mimnaugh

Published by New Generation Publishing in 2024

Copyright © Liam Mimnaugh 2024

First Edition

The author asserts the moral right under the Copyright, Designs and Patents Act 1988 to be identified as the author of this work.

All Rights reserved. No part of this publication may be reproduced, stored in a retrieval system or transmitted, in any form or by any means without the prior consent of the author, nor be otherwise circulated in any form of binding or cover other than that which it is published and without a similar condition being imposed on the subsequent purchaser.

ISBN

    Paperback   978-1-83563-169-0
    Ebook   978-1-83563-170-6

www.newgeneration-publishing.com

Contents

Synopsis 1
Addiction/Alcoholism 2
Introduction 3
Carfin, Scotland – 1980s 4
Newarthill, Scotland – 1990s 7
Newarthill, Scotland – 1996 to 2000 10
Seville – 2002 to 2003 16
Buxton, England – 2000s 18
Stoke, England 20
Kinsale, Ireland 21
Blackpool. England 23
Newarthill, Scotland 24
Catrine, Ayrshire 27
Newarthill, Scotland 28
Faliraki, Greece 29
Newarthill, Scotland 30
Castle Craig, Peebles – Rehab number 2 32
Glasgow, Scotland 34
Glasgow West End. 37
Watford, England – Rehab number 3 38
Watford, England – The Streets 42
Coventry, England (second time) 46
Motherwell, Scotland 47

Newarthill, Scotland 48
Motherwell, Airth Court 49
Mossend, Scotland 54
Aberfeldy, Scotland 58
Dundee, Scotland 59
Fife, Scotland 64
Conclusion 74
Here today and gone tomorrow 79
The last page 80

Synopsis

This is a truth about how my journey with alcohol and drugs took me on a merry dance, an addiction that started way before I put a drink or drug into my body. If the book doesn't show that addiction is an illness and should be treated that way, same as a cancer or a disability can ruin or take a life in the exact same way addiction can.

Sadly in 2023, there is still a big stigma and addicts are treated the same way lepers were back in the days of our Lord, not by everyone, because the book also shows that kindness still exists and it was kindness that got me better. Yes, hospitals, rehabs, etc. got me back on my feet to go again but it was human kindness that got me my life back, and although no names are mentioned, these folks know who they are and I will love and be indebted forever to them all, Thank You!

Addiction/Alcoholism

Addiction/Alcoholism is sadly also treated as a business. There are a lot of people and places making money and taking advantage of addicts. Why make money out of misery? Yes, there are doctors and therapists charging the going rate and doing great jobs, but there are some others who, for what reason I don't know, have to import addicts from other countries and charge crazy money. Are there not enough fucking addicts in every city of Great Britain (my arse)? You can't walk to the shops in this country without meeting or seeing some poor bastard screaming out for help. Loads of sick people with nowhere to go, nowhere to be treated (well unless you meet the right people that is). There are great places like AA and NA etc., but they wouldn't exist if other addicts didn't organize it. It's all fucking wrong and I hope this shows this, but I also want it to give hope.

Introduction

The beginning…this is where the memories, or more like the obsession, began. A small village called "Carfin". Two or three stops on the train one way was Glasgow, and a good few more the other way, was Edinburgh. I won't go too much into these two great Cities yet as they both have big parts to play in the truth, which I am going to share with you all. I am not going to say a story as this is not a story. This is all truth about things in a life that is both comical and deadly serious. Some things that are deadly serious, they are comical. I am choosing to do this now at the age of 43 because, number one, my mother is still alive and luckily dad is too. Mum has always said jokingly that she is going to write a book as she is a big star in my life. Well mum, here it is.

Carfin, Scotland – 1980s

I think my memories begin at aged 4, and even at that age, there is alcohol in those memories; alcohol, football and pubs. Those were the memories in my 4-year-old head, all happy memories though. Oh aye! I nearly forgot Chapel and the Grotto. Have I not mentioned that yet, that me and my family are hardcore Catholic? In fact, Carfin was hardcore Catholic but there was a nice wee story behind why Carfin folks were proud of their Catholic background. Folks from Carfin will happily burn the ear of any man, woman, child or dug that will listen. So, a lot of my memories from then include mass and the Grotto, but by the time I was a teenager, I hated mass and resented going and I will say more later on that. For now, I will start around when I was four.

Football was massive! Carfin Amateurs, my dad Frankie was a bit of a Saturday football legend. The home games played at the Gypsy Park, attracted big crowds. Crowds of locals with their carry outs and bottles of bucky. I was obsessed! That's where I wanted to be. Yes, the football was great and I loved it, but the boys at the side of the park, that's where I wanted to be, and a lot of the time, I ended up there. If my mum was nightshift, I tagged along with my dad, home and away. All of the boys at the side of the park were like babysitters. They all knew me and looked out for me, I loved it.

After the games, we gathered in the Wattfield Bar. This was me truly in heaven. I got crisps and cola and sat in front of the coal fire whilst my dad and his mates got tore into pints and bucky by the glass. I couldn't take my eyes off them. My dad was there for the night and I was raging when mum picked me up. I say raging when mum picked me up because I was. I wanted to stay with the men, the beer, the fire, the pool table and the constant laughing. At that time, the place was thick with fag reek but that didn't put me off. I was happy in amongst it, even if mum wasn't happy, I was there, and before we left, she let dad know, him and his pals. She gave them all pelters too. She wasn't scared of her husband or his pals, not like a lot of women of that era were. In fact, the village next door, their men were called "Cleland Wallopers" because they walloped their women into line, and pretty proud of the nickname. My grandad on my dad's side was one of the most famous wallopers, more about him later on though as he plays a part in this story. Where was I…Yes, mum taking me out the pub.

Even when mum got me home some nights, not them all, my nana, who was dad's gran, aunt Mary and auntie Ann, who were my gran's sisters would be there (my dad's mum, my gran, died very young. My dad had said him and his siblings were brought up in nana's house with Mary, Ann, uncle Sid and grandad William, who I am named after. William had also died by this point). Nana Hana, auntie Mary and Ann were all really close to us and they would come round some nights. Don't get me wrong, me, Danielle my sister and Francis my brother all looked forward to it. They always had sweets but I more noticed the vodka in the other bags. They all enjoyed a wee half in those days, but even at 4, I was drawn to the drink. As I got to 5 and 6, I had gotten braver and stole fly sips. I loved the warm feeling. So, I would say around 6 years old was when I had my first taste.

I am up to around 6 years old now and I had started playing football for a team called Jerviston Boys Club. It's not my local team so this put me in direct competition to a lot of my pals who played for the local team Yett Farm. I was still living in Carfin but me and my sister walked to the next village, Newarthill, so we could be closer to my gran and grandad, Rose and Dan, who helped look after us as dad worked in the Ravenscraig and I think mum was in the passport office, both full time. We went to gran and grandads at lunchtime and after school sometimes.

Football was going well and I was being noticed. My brother Francis made his appearance and we were still in Carfin but mum was looking for a move as the three of us were now in one room and dad had started nailing our teddies to the wall. Honest, he did! Honestly, we came home one day and dad had nailed all our teddies to the wall. Nailed through the ears and feet. We really needed a bigger house and we got a move to a three bedroom in Newarthill, not far from gran and grandad.

Although we moved from Carfin, we still stayed connected. My dad still drank in the Wattfield. In fact, him and mum ran it at one point. We still went to mass there sometimes as I had to go to mass in Newarthill, as this is where I would be getting all my sacraments. We still kept our old pals. In fact, we are still friends with some today but we were based in Newarthill. The bigger house was brilliant. We all got stuck in sorting the garden. I still had to share with Francis but it was still brilliant and we were closer to Dan and Rose.

Newarthill, Scotland – 1990s

The move was good for us to Newarthill. We were all closer to school pals, particularly me, as I had a great bunch of pals. There was Franny and Dougie and we regularly met with a bigger crowd, some older than us by a few years. For big games of football, it was great. All was good, then my granny Rose died. It devastated all of us, especially my grandad. I was the older grandson and had a great relationship with him. In the end, I ended up moving in. He spoke to mum and dad first, then asked me and I jumped at it.

By this time, I was in my early teens and thought of the freedom of it. Just it being me and Dan, excited me. By this time, I was smoking, both fags and weed. It was always easy to get from the older crowd we were now in with and the odd bottle of cider had kicked in as well. I had freedom with Dan, but he had been warned to keep a close eye as he had already caught me drinking and smoking. He had no idea about the weed as he and mum had never experienced that (so they say). All my family were drinkers, never drugs, so I could get away with that to an extent. Dad's punishment for me was a football ban. Stopping me playing hurt me more than any hiding but it just made me more fly. Dan's night out was the local Hibs club, twice a week. When he wasn't there, me and the pals would have wee smoking and drinking sessions, but the house was always spotless for him getting home. I had now started going to Celtic games with a season ticket Dan paid for after giving me pelters for going to watch the Hail Hail Boys as he said.

My football began to take a back seat. I was getting injured and, in the end, a blood disorder that ran in the family had been discovered as the cause. Any teams that were interested in taking me on pro, backed off but I wasn't too devastated, dad and Dan were more hurt. I suppose they had more hope for me getting somewhere in football than I did. I got over it faster with the help of cheap cider and weed. By the time, the full village gathered for sessions in a place called the "Line", which was a place in the middle of the fields. Rain, hail or snow, we were there every weekend. But by this time, I was already dogging school to have afternoon sessions. I was spending this time at my dad's auntie Ann's and my cousins.

My dad was now running a pub called "Scruffy Murphys". My cousin Martin had dosh. My auntie Ann and dad ran the place and me and my cousin hung around drinking. They followed Celtic as well so most weekends I spent with them, still staying at Dans and helping best I could. But, one morning, a Monday, because Dan was out the night before and had come home being sentimental about his daughter Theresa's wedding video. Theresa had just married the year before. I got sent to bed as I had school the next day. Well, I never got up as normal. My pals had been at the door, the dog had been barking but I slept right through until ten. Usually, if I overslept, Dan would wake me but this morning, he couldn't. I found him dead at the bottom of the stairs. Worst day of my life I thought, but more came.

That was the worst day ever but as you will read later, the worse days were coming. The first call I made was an ambulance, then my dad who was there in minutes but it seemed like hours, whilst I tried bringing Dan around but he was stone cold and when the ambulance did turn up, they said he had been dead for hours. Probably not long after I had gone to bed. It looked as if he was trying to get up the stairs, then took a massive heart attack. The poor dog sat with him all night. People told me it was his time, that he missed Rose, blah blah blah. Whatever anyone said, I felt guilty. I was the one meant to be looking after him but instead, he died alone at the bottom of the fucking stairs with only the dog for company. I still carry the guilt today.

Dan was dead and I felt like shit. I had slept through 'til 10:30ish that day. My pals had been ringing the bell, the dog was barking they said, but I slept. Everyone was saying it was his time, blah blah blah, but that didn't make me feel any better. I felt fucking terrible but I found cider and weed made me feel a wee bit better. The pattern started; I can see it now. I think this was the first time I used drink as pain relief. Up until then it was all about having a laugh with my pals, but now it was medicine. Dan's funeral was a blur to be honest. I carried the coffin, said a reading, done all I could. I was only 15 by now. I ended up the Line after it, getting blootered with my pals but even when blootered, I still was guilt ridden. Dan died alone at the bottom of the stairs with the dog for company. The thought is still in my head today. I am now 43. Grief never leaves, you just live with it.

Newarthill, Scotland – 1996 to 2000

I am now coming up to my 16th.birthday. Dan died the December before my 16th birthday. I was still living in Dan and Rose's house. It was the family home and I fought to stay. North Lanarkshire Council thought I was pretending to live with Dan so we could keep the house. I had to get letters of proof from the priest and the school to back me up but the bampots still threw me out. Mum and dad wanted me to go back home. No fucking chance! I had freedom no other 16-year-old in Newarthill ever had. I had got used to doing my own shit. I had no one to sneak past half pished. I could look after myself if I could cook, iron, clean blah blah blah. I didn't need to go back. The council made me a deal. They agreed to give me a smaller house right next to the Hibs club. Ya dancer! But then dad brought me down with a bang. "You better get a job cause I can't keep 2 houses". Me being the stubborn prick I am said fine, I would get a job, and I did. A pal's dad was high up with a construction company and I got a start working with the engineer on the new Eurocentral at Newhouse, about 15-20 minutes' walk from the house, I got a lift. I had the house, the job, fucking minted! I worked hard and partied harder. I got paid on a Thursday. Good money, I was on about £350 a week which was brilliant. When I wasn't working with the engineer, I would help with the concrete pours. I got tore in and it was noticed. I was offered an apprenticeship.

By this time, I was smoking weed at work, sometimes a sneaky couple of cans if I was rough. I was getting a bottle of bucky on the way home and I was getting a few beers at night. Now, at 17, I was on it most nights. I hadn't even noticed my mum and dad were still keeping an eye on me. Mum had a key and had a bad habit of turning up and chucking folks out. Sometimes, I would come home blootered and mum and my sister would be sitting waiting on me like freaky fucking ghosts. Dad would turn up in the Hibs or the Wattfield as I had started venturing to Carfin, thinking I could hide there, but everyone knew me and it got back to mum and dad.

Dad was buzzing that I had been offered the apprenticeship joiner. He thought a trade sets you up for life. He shoveled shit all his days as he put it and would have cut his arm off to be offered one when he was younger, but it was a big drop in wages and by this time, I had a couple of habits. I took it in the end.

Bang! One week, £350, next week £80 and that was with travel expenses. Fuck, what had I done. I had to get another earner. First stop was the bank. I applied for a loan and credit card but I was only 17. I filled the forms and changed my date of birth from 1980 to 1979. The stupid bastards gave me it and for a year, I got away with it, just! Paying the minimum and upping the credit limit, remember I told you mum had a key, well that one bit me right in the arse. I had left my bank statements out and she read them. Mum being mum, she went right down to the bank and stuck me in for being 17, not deliberately. She thought she was helping. The bank phoned the police and I was charged but I was off on one last blowout. Coventry, here I come! Nobody knew for 3 weeks where I was. I turned up at my dads' sisters in Coventry. She had been there for years and had made a home there. She covered for me for 3 weeks but in the end, it was killing her lying to my mum and dad. I went home to face the music. The polis actually had a wee chuckle to themselves. In a way, they were impressed I had fooled the bank for over a year and if mum hadn't been involved, I probably would have for longer.

I got back to work, still getting stoned during the day and drunk at night. I sold a bit of weed to get by and done homers. I was now 19 and an opportunity had come up to buy the house and clear some debt. I got the house for about

£19,000 approximately, nearly half price. The house was valued at more, so I got a wee bit extra to clear the debt of the dodgy loan. My time was nearly served.

I will press pause here, just to recap. I have moved from Carfin, to Newarthill, where I spent my time between mum and dads and gran and grandads. I had a good upbringing apart from a spell over a couple of years at primary school when a family friend took advantage of how welcoming my grandparents were, and used this to abuse me. I will not go into this as it's a sore one for the family.

Gran and grandad were now dead. I found my grandad dead and was now riddled with grief and guilt. I didn't go back to mum and dads after grandad died. I thought I was Johnny big balls and took a house on. I am now serving my time as a joiner. I have a fraud charge against me, which was dropped as it was bad press for the bank. I have now gone on to buy my council house with a big discount, which meant I got a decent mortgage. The mortgage gave me enough to clear the debt I had run up and got me on my feet. I was now in the last year of my apprenticeship. My house was party central. I used to go to work and leave my pals in the house still partying. A couple of people even had keys. I was now drinking every day. I had a van of guys who were ground workers from Airdrie. They used to pick me up in the morning with a carry out. Fuck knows how I never got sacked. As if drink and weed wasn't enough, the powder now began getting passed about, speed not coke. It sobered you up enough to get your shift done and get back home to the party, but the suicidal down with speed was not good for someone already suffering with mega guilt.

My usual week was work, I always made work whatever nick I was in. Payday was Thursday, so the rest of the week was boozing at home but a Thursday was the pub, then Faces nightclub in Motherwell. Full of underage folks, we would always walk it home, 3-4 miles, and we always (well most of the time) ended up fighting with boys from other villages. One time we go to my house and some of the boys we were fighting with were at my door. This ended up with a riot in my front garden. One of my best mates, and to this day, still a best mate, and trust me there's not many left, well he nearly ripped the door off a car to get to a boy who he battered in the back seat. They scarpered and we got into my house. My pal's shirt was covered in blood, so he wanted a shirt to change into. I told him to help himself. Problem here is, he is well built and I am a skinny dude. When he put the shirt on, he was bursting out it like the hulk. We couldn't laugh long though as the street was now crawling with police. They chapped a few doors, but to this day, I will never know why they didn't chap mines. They chapped one neighbours' door, who had seen everything. He liked a good bevvy as well and we had a good laugh about it. Incidents like this were becoming common. One time another workmate had been arrested outside Faces over an argument with a girl. His car was parked at mines. I thought it was a good idea to take it out a run with a drink in me. Only one pal was daft enough to come with me. Poor guy is now passed. Gem of a guy. It turned out the roads were pretty icy and the only driving experience I had was a dumper truck at work. My mate talked me into driving home but turning into my street, I hit the ice and went right through my neighbour's fence. In the panic, trying to reverse out we hit a pole. We managed to park up and get to mine. All the time, my drug dealer was waiting for me and had witnessed all of this. My mates back lights were mangled but that didn't matter. We were sat waiting for a chap from the polis, but again, I got away with it. The next morning my neighbour stopped me. I thought I was busted but he was asking me to fix the fence I had reversed through myself. I couldn't say no and when he wanted to pay me, I had to take it to keep up the pretense. I got it stinking for that.

When the guy who owned the car got out the cells, he came for his car and seen the damage. I played dumb but he knew deep down what had happened. He was too nice to pull me up but I was out of order. My mum had noticed how mad my life was and more importantly, I was by now, far gone with the drink. Especially as she has seen alcoholism on both her and my dad's side. One family of 4 brothers on mums' side, all alcoholics. Some still on it and some in AA. Dads side had a family who had twins. Both dead by the time they were not even 40 years old. So, mum was qualified enough to spot I was fucked. But my reply was, "I work hard, I deserve a drink, it's not me who has the problem but everyone else who has the problem with me drinking so more or less fuck off, don't waste my fun and it helps me forget".

There were plenty of good nights in that house. One Christmas Eve, we ran a bus to Room at the Top, a nightclub in Bathgate. At the end of the night, we were waiting on a couple of the guys held up in the coat queue and the bus driver was threatening to leave. My pal had other ideas and stole the bus keys. The driver called the police who turned up and escorted us back to Newarthill. The delay tactic worked as nobody missed the bus and we all got home, but when I turned up at mums that Christmas morning, she sent me away again. Looking back, there were loads of us that all ran around together, a really good bunch of pals. That's another thing the drink cost me, a load of good friendships. None ended in bad terms and I still speak to most of them today, but drink and drugs took me one way and them another. They all were and still are good boys.

I still had a lot of pain from the abuse and guilt from Dan dying. In my eyes, I had let him down. But my fun plan was about to look in jeopardy. I was soon to become a dad. This never stopped the party. In a way, it made it worse. It was as if I was trying to party as much as I could before the wean was born. That's what I told everyone, I would "calm down when the wean was born". Bullshit! I wet that weans head for 10 years. The wean came the year I turned 20 and my time as a joiner was due to be served. I was on good money so the wean wanted for nothing. It was cramped in the house but one night, when the wean was nearly 1, I got a chap at the door. A woman wanted to buy my house. She asked me for a price. I done my sums, I paid £19k, my mortgage was £32k, I added £10k and said to her £42k. Deal done! Ya dancer! £10k profit approximately. The wean's mum had been on the housing list so she got offered a house but I had no intention of moving in. I paid to do it up and ended up buying it but me and a guy who I had teamed up with, we had planned to go to England to a place called Buxton, building a cement works. It was 12-hour shifts and about £800 a week. Happy days! I travelled down in the back of a small transit van, no window etc. I didn't give a shit, I had a bottle and eight cans, a healthy lump of weed and a piss bottle. The guy I teamed up with was a coke dealer as well and pretty wild. The other passenger was just as bad as he actually smoked coke. So, I was an alcoholic/addict in great company…let the fun begin!

Seville

Thie year, Celtic got to the UEFA cup final in Seville. I had to get there. It was out first Euros final since 1967, a once in a lifetime thing. The thing was, travel agents were taking funny money. They knew they would get it. I gambled and hung off 'til the last minute and got a deal for 7 days. Flights only, no hotel for £199. I couldn't say no, so me and a pal's wee brother booked the flight, was into Malaga. So, we took a rucksack and locked the rest of our stuff in an airport locker. We still had about a 12-hour bus journey. It was party central. All the Spanish boys were out selling coke, hash etc., so before we got on the bus to Seville, we scored a bit hash. This turned out to be the costliest bit ever because the fucking dealer robbed my mate's wallet. We never realised until we were on the bus halfway to Seville. It had his money and his plane ticket etc. What a fucking disaster!

When we got to Seville, we booked into a hostel. My mate's sister put money in my bank for him so that was the first thing we sorted. We would deal with the place ticket later. The second night, we met up with a load of pals who were booked into a caravan park with a pool, so we crashed with them for a couple of nights. The night of the game, we met my mate they had a gig the night of the game. We met them and helped them get set up. I actually woke up in the park they had to play the gig in. I was well blootered by now. Four solid days on it. It was about 100 degrees as well so I was like Buster Bloodvessel. All that I remember about the night of the game, was watching it on the big screen. There were folks up lamp posts, on portacabins, it was mayhem. We got beat but by fuck, we partied and the Spanish loved us.

The next day, we said cheerio to our pals who had only booked for 3 nights, but me being me, ripped the arse out it and booked for 7 nights. No digs remember, so we had to rough it 2 nights. There were plenty other stragglers to have a bevvy with and that's what I did for 2 nights. By now, I had lost my mate who was panicking about his lost ticket so he went to the airport to sort it. We met up the day of our flight home. The airport was like the walking dead. Folks too pished to fly. In fact, on our flight, the Spanish police escorted one guy home. I think by now, the Spanish wanted their town back. That day we got home and straight to the pub to watch Celtic lose the league to Rangers on goal difference. What a week! I spent a few days rattling after that week.

Buxton, England – 2000s

Buxton was a small town. The whole town was dependent on the cement works and we were there to build a new one. The new cement works was a massive job, about 2000+ men, and the old one was operated, so it was a busy town. We moved into a house on a street the locals called "little Scotland", because one landlord owned the full street and rented them out, 2 men sharing a room. The guy I shared with was from Airdrie, not far from Carfin but this was the first time I met him. I could tell her was an arsehole from day 1 and he turned out to be worse than an arsehole. He was a bully but he never tried it with me because of my mate who was well handy, so nobody gave us shit. My mate had a reputation and everyone knew how handy he was. He did illegal fighting for cash.

We travelled to work on double decker buses that left at 6:30am from a car park about 10 minutes from the cement works. We done 12-hour shifts but there was always drink and coke getting passed around so they flew by quicker. We could afford it as the wages were brilliant. After work, we were straight to a pub called "The Cheshire Cheese". The landlord loved us because it was like a lottery win for him. We spent a fortune there. The locals fucking hated our guts though. They were jealous and to be fair, we were flash with our cash. The town had a nightclub that was open until 3am, so we always ended up there, and most nights, we ended up fighting with the locals (winning most of the time because as I said, my mate was very handy).

To begin with, we always made work because we needed the money, but the late nights took their toll and we ended up missing shifts. That was ok because by this time, the boy I shared with and my mate, were doing trips to Manchester to buy large amounts of coke to sell to the other 2000+

workers. Well, a good percentage of them anyway. The missing work was not going down well and we were starting to get warnings. Plus, the locals were starting to really hate us so it was time to go home. We had planned to go in a week but we got broken into by one of the boys who had been sacked. I didn't lose anything apart from clothes and aftershave, but the silly bastard who robbed us, got caught and battered.

The boy ended up hospitalised. I wasn't involved but my mate was. The police got involved but there ended up being no charges as the guy had robbed us all but agreed to drop the charges if he was allowed to get away safely. Anyway, we had all outstayed our welcome. It was time to go and we all went home and went our separate ways. I had no intention of going home and having the family life this time. I took another job away from home. I got started with a company in Cleland. My dad knew the owner. We were travelling to England, building clean rooms for laboratory, medical science, etc. Again, another great paying job and the freedom of being away from home. I still provided for my kid and paid the mortgage.

Stoke, England

I am saying Stoke. The first place I worked building the clean rooms was close to Stoke. I have actually forgot the name of the place. I knew most of the boys working with me and the same old pattern continued. Work hard, drink hard, take coke to keep you going and I really needed the coke by now. If I didn't do the coke, I would fall over with the drink and then I couldn't work and earn. I needed to work as by now, I had 2 expensive habits plus a kid and a mortgage to pay at home. We travelled all over England building clean rooms. At one point, we ended up on a ferry to a place called Kinsale, just outside of Cork, Ireland, on the coast of one of the most beautiful places I have ever been.

Kinsale, Ireland

Kinsale was a tiny fishing port, south of Cork. Right at the very bottom of Ireland. We got there by ferry, to Belfast and then a drive that took all day because the lot of us were blootered and we had to pull in for piss stops every hour. It was late by the time we got to Kinsale. We were booked into a couple of houses, really nice digs. That was the other great thing about this job, we were always in nice accommodation. We got up as usual about 6am, had breakfast and then drove to the job. We got stopped abruptly by 2 security guards and spent the rest of the day sitting in the van in the car park. This job was on an army base and it being Ireland, we all needed clearance. You would think they would know that.

We were instructed by the foreman that night, that we would have to get up for work as normal at 6am. We would wait for word of getting security clearance and if we don't get cleared by 12 noon, then the rest of the day was our own to do what we wanted to do. Keep in mind, there was a dozen guys who would all need cleared before we could start the job. Well, this was a result for us. It went on for a full month and from 12 noon onwards, we were off the leash. Kinsale was beautiful. It was all tourism and fishing, so that's what we all acted like, fucking tourists. It was the middle of summer. It must have been at least 25-39 degrees. We bought a football and some fishing gear and that's how we spent our days. Each day, it would strike 12 noon and it was a slab of lager and a bottle of Irish Buckfast, which was a lot more sugary than the Scottish Buckfast I had drank since I was 13 years old but I got used to it. We sat at the harbour fishing or played football. That was being a tourist to me, but Kinsale was full of Americans and Chinese doing their tourist things. At night, we would do a pub crawl then a nightclub, or Cork a few times for a change of scenery. This went on for a month and we were getting paid. We had made a contact Cork to get coke from. So, between that the all-day drinking, there wasn't much wage left. One day, out of the blue, we were told the Irish party was over and we were to go home for a week. Then it was Blackpool.

Blackpool. England

Blackpool was a brilliant set up. The company booked out a full guest house next door to the Pleasure Beach and casino right across the road. You could buy buckfast in Blackpool no bother. We were also fed. The woman who owned the house gave us bed and dinner, so we were well sorted. We also found out if you were a casino member, that you could get your beer for nothing. On certain nights, there was a buffet on so we spent most nights there. We would take £50 with us and gamble with it, blackjack or roulette usually. If we won, then brilliant but if we lost, we weren't too bothered. We were getting free drink and then move on to clubs etc. In total, we were 9 months in Blackpool. A few times we were sent to Liverpool but we done the exact same thing; work, drink and coke.

As you can see, up to now there are loads of places mentioned, but my life was the same pattern – work hard and party harder. Something had to come to a head. My body could only take so much and one night, it gave in on me. We had been out one Wednesday, had a big win on the casino roulette and I ended up in a club. I took some pills on top of my usual drink and coke, and I collapsed inside the club. I had to be resuscitated and woke up in hospital with my boss stood over me. His exact words were, "So, I am not sacking you but I want you to take a month off and rest up, and your dad would agree". Him and dad knew each other from back in the day. So, I was sent home feeling total shite. My body felt as if it had taken a good kicking.

Newarthill, Scotland

During my month rest up, I just spent my days in the pub catching up with the old friends. My mum, who was as I said, well-tuned in when it came to alkies, had started to get on my case about going to AA. I had moved into the house I had been paying for and had been told I was going to be a dad again. I only ever used the house to get washing done and get my head down in between work and the pub. I thought I was a great dad as I was still throwing a lot of money at my kids' mum. After my month off, I met a guy who I had worked under when serving my apprenticeship. We had been given a contract to erect and fit out kit houses for a well-known builder. It meant going self-employed and being my own boss.

Being self-employed meant putting and keeping a van on the road, our own tools etc. My mate did all the driving as the van was his. This suited me as I had never drove, except a dumper or fork lift. Thank God I never got a driving license. I would have killed myself or some other poor bugger. We also started a laborer. It all worked out great. In the couple of years doing it, we must have made at least 100 grand each and I needed it. My 2 habits were now through the rood. We used to get paid approximately every 10 days. We were on a price and got paid per house. Every 10 days, we would get a cheque for approximately £3000 each. We chipped in about £300 each for the labourer. Every time we were paid, we had to cash the cheque and pay the labourer. Then I got dropped off at my local. My coke dealer would be waiting and he got paid, I got more coke and then the party began. The staying at home came to an abrupt end after one massive bender. I went home and argued with the kids' mum, the police got phoned and I got lifted. When putting me in the van, I threw my head back and connected with the bridge of the copper's nose. As you can expect, he was fucking raging! I got charged with police assault and was put in front of a judge. I was bailed and part of the conditions were, I was not allowed near the house I was still paying for. I had to move in with a pal. He had a big coke habit as well.

Staying with my pal was good and I was grateful but the parties were starting to affect my work, or as I would like to say, my work was getting in the way of my partying. By now, I was getting access to my kids every odd weekend. I had a girl and a boy now. I would pick them up from my mum and dads. I would leave money with my dad for the kids. He made their mum sign for it as she was bad mouthing me saying I wasn't providing, so dad made her sign. Mum was always getting in my ear about AA. She was persistent at the time and it infuriated me but being a sober parent now, I can see the hell I was inflicting on her and anyone else connected to me. But I thought in my sick head, I worked hard so I was entitled to relax, leave me alone!

Another good friend of dad's gave me around £3000 to pay a tax bill but that went on drink and coke. That's the way things were going, ripping folks off, bumping loans, all my tools ended up pawned. It took me a long time to build up my tool kit. I needed it all to earn but it was all gone in one afternoon. I was getting closer to the gutter every day, lower and lower.

My pal, who I lived with, had to give up his house. Me and him moved in with his mum on the same street as the one mum kids lived. I had to keep my head down as I was breaking my bail conditions being there. The guy I worked with was by now pissed off with the way I was living so we went our separate ways. I teamed up with my old pal from Buxton. I put a van and car on the road as the job was in a place called Catrine in Ayrshire. Now was the start of everything coming down and round about me. I travelled up and down to Ayrshire every day, always with a carry out.

The labourers were more like drivers and one day, I went too far and pissed my pal right off.

Catrine, Ayrshire

Catrine was a tiny wee village. The job was a block of flats on the same site of an old brewery with a pub around the corner. I spent my time there. I was working 'til 11:00am and then spending the rest of the day sitting in the pub. The labourers I had been leaving on the job were not the best and the job was getting behind. My pal was getting pissed off big time as he was the middleman between us and the big bosses. When this pal was annoyed, he was dangerous. One day, I never even waited 'til 11:00am. I just drove about Ayrshire, drinking and snorting. My pal had passed us on the road and got us to pull into a layby. He came storming right up to me and knocked me right out with a left hook. We still stayed pals after that.

Newarthill, Scotland

By this time, the pal I was staying with, was having problems with his mum. It wasn't fair on her. By now, I was working cash in hand for a local company, the money was gone. I had pawned a load of my tools to cover my coke habit. One of the other guys who lived with his mum, suggested moving into a house of a friend of his. We moved in there, split the rent and spent most of our time when not working, sitting drinking and snorting. His mum fed us as we were both no on good wages. So, one day I got a tax rebate from my time being self-employed. The days of earning big money were long gone, so when I got this tax rebate, I booked 2 weeks all-inclusive in Faliraki, Greece. This was the beginning of the end for me. This holiday brough things to a head.

Faliraki, Greece

We arrived in Faliraki, steaming drunk. We had smuggled a wee bit coke to keep us going until we found more. The first day of the holiday, I fell asleep at the pool and got fucking roasted. A nice family pulled me under a tree, thank fuck of I would have been hospitalised. The first night, me and my pal got wrecked and ended up having what I call, "a square go". This nightly square go happened a few times. We spent most of the holiday going about with black eyes. The night we were due to leave, we missed our airport taxi. Some friends we had made from Liverpool had taken us out. I think they actually wanted us to miss our flight. We ended up in total, 3 weeks in Faliraki. My mate's brother put the extra on the credit card. On the flight home, I physically shook coming off the drink. I had decided, I was moving out too.

Newarthill, Scotland

Mum, you were right! I was fucked with the drink. It wasn't a choice anymore. On that flight home, I admitted it to myself for the first time, I think. Even though if I am being honest, I had known many years earlier, but at that time, there was still fun. There was no fun anymore. My body was needing it now, screaming for it. The incidents were getting more serious. Fuck, I had just been stranded in another country with a guy I didn't like and had to fight off. I moved in with mum and her being mum, had put me in touch with AA and a rehab called "Phoenix Futures". It was a daily rehab. I attended daily but I stayed with mum and dad. I was still drinking on the side and running up coke bills but still, I went every day.

I was in mum's spare room, still drinking. I was stealing it, raiding the copper jars and borrowing from pals. I had cut down on the coke. Drink was more important. Mum and dad couldn't work out how I was managing it as they thought they were keeping an eye on me. I was taking more risks. Everything of value got pawned. I had gone from being the boss to taking odd cash in hand jobs. On one occasion, mum was getting her kitchen fitted and the poor guy took the cupboards off the wall and got his with a pile of strong cans, all empty of course. Mum just told the guy straight, "my son's an alky. He was staying here and we couldn't work out how he was getting drink every day. Now I know!" Typical alky, I always found a way to get drink. If only I had the same commitment to getting better. I never stole off my mum, dad or sister but shops were fair game, victimless crime. I told myself to make me feel better that their insurance would cover their losses. All bullshit of course! But I needed to drink so I always found a way. One time, I couldn't pay a £140 coke bill. My dealer picked up another boy with a £100 bill. He was going to forget his bill in return for stabbing me. It never happened! I just got a few slaps. But fuck's sake, it was all gone! I was on my arse. It was around this time I first took a shit load of pills, washed with cheap cider and had ended up in hospital.

Castle Craig, Peebles – Rehab number 2

Whilst in hospital, mum and one of the workers from Phoenix Futures (the first rehab place I went to) got their heads together with another worker from Motherwell. Social work had managed to get me a place in "Castle Craig", a private rehab in Peebles, close to the Scottish Borders. This place was £600 a day. Folks like me never got in there. I don't know how mum managed but she got her teeth into them and they gave in and I got a place. There was the odd Scottish person in there, but most were Dutch. We found out that their insurance policies paid for their stay. This caused friction as they treated it like a holiday. We Scottish folks got £20 a week spending money to shop in Peebles on a Saturday for essentials and the Dutch were going on spending sprees. It was causing problems.

In Castle Craig, you done a detox in a room with about half a dozen others. You got valium and Librium to help with the withdrawals but it was torture. When you were over the worst, you spent the day doing one-to-one therapy, group therapy and at night, they put you in a minibus and took you to AA and NA meetings. But as I said, there was tension as all the Scottish folks knew people on the outside who were dying and would be desperate for a place here. There was drinking going on and always a bit dope on the go, but I stayed away from the drink. I took a smoke. We got searched when we came home from meetings. We found out folks were filling condoms with vodka and sneaking it in that way. Genuis if you think of it but alkies are resourceful.

Another thing that got to me in Castle Craig was there were a lot of American soldiers. If they stepped out of line and the incident was drink related, they either got sent to army jail or rehab. More money getting made from misery. They openly admitted that rehab was an easy choice, a nice wee

3 month break in the Scottish countryside. All I could think of were my alky pals I had left back home. They were dying and the place I was in was acting as a holiday for spoilt soldiers from thousands of miles away. There was no way this place would work for me. All it did was fill me with anger and resentment. No offence to America, they are bigger, richer and have more facilities. Why use a Scottish rehab to treat babied soldiers? I am sorry, Scotland is full of dying men and women, dads, mums, brothers and sisters.

Castle Craig was paid for on a 6-month basis and my funding had run out. Out of all my pals, there were a handful left. Two great guys in particular who I am still pals with, used to visit me and encourage me. I knew I was being turfed out. Pals I had made there had got the hat round. So, the day, I was leaving, I ended up with a few quid. I had decided to go to Glasgow as I had debts in Newarthill I didn't want to deal with. I had decided I was going to Glasgow the day I left Castle Craig. I got dropped off in Peebles and within 5 minutes, I was sitting in a bus stop with a bottle of buckfast and a few tins of cider. I sat there and waited on the pub opening, then sat in the pub 'til closing time. Then I got the last train to Glasgow where I booked into a hostel.

Glasgow, Scotland

Fuck knows what I was thinking. What I had learned from my stint in Castle Craig, and from my mum, was that AA are like a big gang and you can get help there. So, the first place I went to, was an AA meeting. After speaking to a few folks, I had multiple offers of digs, I had a choice of where to stay. In the end, I first went to stay with a guy and his girlfriend but there were trying to stay sober. It wasn't fair on these good folks who were trying to do their own 12 step program by helping me. In the end, I left them. No hard feelings. I ended up sofa surfing around the AA people's homes but all this was temporary. I had by now, registered as homeless. You turned up at this place each afternoon. If you were lucky, you got a bed in a hostel, if not, you got a sleeping bag. I was now officially homeless. How the fuck did this happen to me?

This was the start of my being homeless in Glasgow. If you were one of the ones who got a sleeping bag, the best place was to go to a rail bridge or motorway flyover and hang about down there. It was busy and to be fair, everyone helped everyone. If someone had a giro, it was shared about. If they had a drink, it was shared. They knew where to go to a soup kitchen to get some food. At least everyone was a seasoned shoplifter, me included by now. You'd walk into a shop, get your order on the counter, your pal held the door and you ran as fast as you could, being careful not to drop a can. A simple but effective way of getting by. You got barred from every shop in the end. Supermarkets were next. Even better, because you didn't need anyone to hold the door.

In some ways, you were safer under a bridge. You would think you were lucky getting a bed in a hostel, but it was the opposite. Folks in there would try and rob you. My survival technique was, I could make pals, I could get along with folks and I knew which pals to keep and ones to avoid. The hostels were dangerous places and I found out big time. One weekend I was sharing a place in Govan, right outside my favourite place, Ibrox. This place was crazy! It was mixed and even the women would "square go" the men. Most of the fighting was over tobacco, drugs or drink. I was sharing a flat with a guy and we got on. Well, speed was his thing and everyone kind of left him alone which meant I got left alone. One weekend he had been taking speed and hardly slept. I was my usual drunk. I found out why the rest of the hostel avoided my mate I shared with. He had mental health issues. One weekend after a lot of speed and drink, right out of the blue, with absolutely no warning, he jumped from his seat and kicked me clean in the face. He then proceeded to kick and jump on my head until he was disturbed by someone coming into the flat. He then sat down on his seat and carried on playing his computer game, whilst I lay in a heap with a broken jaw and a fractured eye socket. The crazy thing is, I still sat the rest of the weekend drinking with this nutter because he had the carry out. My blood was up the walls. The staff knew what had gone on and I was asked if I wanted the police involved but absolutely no way could I be known as a grass.

At the start of the following week, I had arranged to see my mum and the kids. Mum burst into tears and my kids wouldn't come near me. I was black and blue and could hardly walk. The visit ended quickly. When I got back to the hostel, there was a taxi waiting. I was being moved to a different hostel, this time in Glasgow's West End, the posh part of Glasgow. This was stuck right in the middle of million-pound houses. I was sharing this time with a cracking guy whose mum had kicked him out. He took a drink but preferred his guitar. We would sit and jam and he looked out for me. I was beginning to take seizures and a few times, he went and got me the best cure for seizures, a can of cider, lager or whatever. It may not sound like looking after me but at this time, he was a true pal.

Glasgow West End.

This hostel was the Ritz of hostels. The staff were good and my flat mate was good. My mum was on the scene always bringing pamphlets about other rehabs etc. They all got filed in the top drawer. One day, my 2 best pals visited and took me for a fish supper, which in Glasgow's West End, isn't cheap. This show of kindness was like giving me a million pounds. They also left me a few quid as I had told them I had been shoplifting. They couldn't believe where I had ended up and neither could I. I was fucked! I had the shakes every morning. I need drink and a lot of it and sometimes I couldn't get it. I took a bad seizure one night and the staff called me an ambulance and my mum, who then turned up at the hospital with my younger brother.

When mum turned up, my brother took me out for a smoke. Outside, all he done was nip my head about giving up drinking blab blah blah. This resulted in another square go with me and my brother rolling about outside A&E like a couple of 5-year-olds with my poor mum in the middle. Hospital security eventually separated us. When things calmed down, my mum pushed a phone number under my nose for a place in Watford, a rehab. I agreed to make the call and they said I could get in. All I had to do was get there. Mum got my auntie to buy a ticket on the train for me but I wasn't going quietly. I blackmailed them into getting me a carry out for the train. I got blootered and a couple I got talking to, called the rehab people to meet me.

Watford, England – Rehab number 3

I was met off the train at Watford Junction by 2 guys who were nice enough. I got outside the train station, got my tobacco pouch out to roll a fag and one of the guys grabbed the pouch off me and said "we don't smoke here". I thought "what the fuck! I'm expected to give up fags and the drink?" What have I done? I talked them into giving it to a homeless guy sat at the train station begging. It was a full pouch of Golden Virginia; I couldn't bin it. The homeless guy thought we had given him a million quid. That's the thing when you are homeless, the slightest bit of kindness is well appreciated. I've been there! Anyway, I got put in the car and got taken to a house right on the outskirts of the centre of Watford. "How's this going to work?" I was thinking…

The house was cracker and I got searched. My phone etc. was confiscated. They chucked me into a shower. The 2 guys waited in the actual toilet with me. Fuck knows what they thought I was going to do in the shower, but they stood there. I was that drunk, I fell in the shower so the 2 guys helped me out and patched me up with butterflies. They gave me clean clothes because they said mine stank of booze and fags, and that the other residents may smell it and it sets them off the rails. I got led to a bedroom with about 10 bunks with other guys in it. I got given a set of drawers and a bedside lamp. I was told they would wash my clothes and give me them back. My mum had put some prayers in my bag and they took these also. Strange one that!

We all got kicked out of bed at 6am. We gathered into a big living room. There was a small stage set up with a mic and a keyboard, "WHAT THE FUCK?!" Next, 3 guys and a girl took the stage and everyone stood up. They all began singing gospel songs, everyone clapping along. I was in shock and was already planning my getaway. There were also 2 kids kicking about. This place was strange…a fucking rehab with kids? After 30-40 minutes singing and clapping, we all had breakfast and the guys split into 3 groups. They all got given a packed lunch, 2 slices of ham or chicken and a bag of crisps. Group 1 was off to a furniture warehouse; group 2 were going to do landscaping and group 3 were away to hand out flyers' door to door.

I was left at the house with 2 other guys. We were there to do housework, get everyone's washing done and to make the dinner for the rest coming home. I was rattling by now bug time, but there was no valium in here or lying down. I got handed 2 paracetamol and a tattie peeler and given a big bag of tatties to peel. I could hardly hold the fucking thing. I found by talking to the 2 bodyguards left with me that this rehab was called Betel, that it had houses all over the UK. Most of these houses were donated and they actually had houses all over Europe. They also had a furniture warehouse. The group doing the flyers were advertising free furniture collections and landscaping services. They had this set up all over the UK.

I had landed my sorry arse in a second rehab that was being run as a business. The girl and the kids lived in a flat about the house. They were the managers. The house was full of recovering addicts and alcoholics. This was big business. After 2 weeks doing the worst rattle of my life, I was fucking seeing things and everything, but I got through it. Fuck knows how with no fags or anything. I had already started my get out of here plan. I had worked out by now why my prayers and holy medals were confiscated. This place was protestant. They sand and clapped about God and Jesus all day long but any mention of any Saints was a no-go area. That was OK though, me being brought up Catholic, I could use this to my advantage and I knew I could. My first job was handing out the flyers. We walked about for 8 fucking hours sticking flyers in letterboxes.

Over the course of the first 3 months, I got a shot of working in the furniture warehouse where you were sometimes out collecting. If it wasn't the best of stuff and they couldn't sell it, it would be collected. But this was London remember, so they did end up with the best of stuff. They actually had a well-known auction house, dropping their scraps into us once a month, and talking scraps, we never paid a penny for grub. Twice a week we stopped in at Sainsburys to pick up a van load of food, plenty for all of us. All we had to do was cook it. When we worked in the garden group, it wasn't mowing pissy wee lawns. It was thousands worth of landscaping. All we got out of it was our dinner. We also visited different "churches" around Britain. I had worked out by now that this was a money-making, well-run business not fucking rehab.

It pissed me off that this rehab was using people's misery to make money and I was making plans. After 3 months, we were allowed a visitor. Mum and dad flew down for the day and what a performance the higher up members put on. They made a massive Sunday roast. My dad loved it that much he had to have a wee kip after it. I found him crashed out on a couch in the games room. It gave me and my mum a chance to talk and for me to plant a seed in her brain. When I told her how the rehab was run as a business and that they were confiscating the holy medals and prayers card she had been sending, it pissed her right off. She and dad flew back home raging. The first part of my getaway plan was hatched. Also, the fact that the rehab was protestant really got to mum. I carried on. I actually got a lot out of the hard work. I enjoyed it and it was satisfying but I still wanted out.

I stuck it out another few months but enough was enough. In amongst the guys I met, were guys who had been in the Betel rehab movement for 8-9 years. One guy had been in there hiding from the IRA all that time. No fucking way was that being me. I put the second part of my get out plan into action. I convince my mum to send a postal order. I had convinced her I could find work doing my joinery. I told her I had made contacts that could set me up, all a load of bullshit but because of the protestant thing I had already planted and the fact it was a business, mum had a big heart. Especially for alkies and addicts. She thought making money out of misery was all wrong and she was correct, of course it was wrong. So, when I got home one night to find a card from the post office saying I had a parcel, that was me. Next morning, I was off.

Watford, England – The Streets

Instead of getting up at 6am to go downstairs to sing and clap, I got up and packed my bag. The Irish guy tried to talk me out of it but him talking to me made me more determined. They gave me £2 for a phone call and gave me back my phone and I demanded my mum's holy medals and prayers. I left and had a good walk to the post office to collect my parcel. I had plans for my £2 and as soon as 10am came, I was into the closest off license to buy myself a nice cold can of Stella. I had been waiting months for this and it went down a treat. When I did get to the post office, there was some clothes, a £150 postal order and some holy medals of course. It wasn't a bad start. It would keep me going until I could get my benefits up and running again. I took a ruck sack with essentials and locked the rest in a locker at the station.

I needed to find somewhere to stay and somewhere to eat. I had been here before and I knew who would help me out and it wasn't the social. The best folk for me was the folks the same as me. Watford was a big place. Loads of pubs and clubs and a big shopping centre. I had to find where the street drinkers sat around. I found them easy, in the big park outside a Cathedral I think, if not, a big Church. As soon as I sat down on a bench with a bag of strong cans, that was me in. And as soon as they heard the Scottish accent, I was right in. That day, I experience real kindness. There was a load of guys but 2 in particular walked me all round Watford, showing me a soup kitchen to get a feed at 1-m and 7pm each day. They showed me the social. Both places I needed and they did not need to do that, but they did.

I know I am not putting names in here, but one of the guys that day that helped me out for no gain to himself was called Papa Smurf. An old guy who looked about 70 but was probably only 50. He had an old bogging bomber jacket and a wooly hat. He had been homeless for 23 years. Poor old guy was street hardened. It was the cheap cider that kept him alive. I hardly saw him eat but 23 years he was at this shite. The fact no one had reached out to help him was even worse. That night, we all slept in that big park next to the big Church. The reason they chose there was simple, the Church got all lit up at night. There was a skateboard ramp and plenty of room for us all and a wee fire. I had only known these guys a few hours and they were treating me like a brother. It was always the ones with fuck all.

When I went to the social, I got lucky. The first guy at the door was the meet and greet guy. He took me aside. I explained everything. He told me the first thing I had to do was get a letter from the rehab because my claim got stopped because I disappeared off the face of the earth and I had missed a medical back in Glasgow. I had to go back to the rehab and ask them to help me out. We hadn't left on the best terms but luckily, they gave me a letter. I handed it back to my new pal at the social who got the ball rolling. He sorted me out a crisis loan, and I went back to Papa Smurf and the others, drinks were on me. My pal at the social told me to keep my eyes open for a room in a house, as when my claim was started, I could claim housing benefit. This was London, so it was easier said than done.

The went on for a couple of weeks. I had no phone call from my pal at the social, so I went back in. My crisis loan had run out and I was back to stealing booze. When I got him, he was very apologetic. He told me to take a seat and went upstairs. He came back smiling about 45 minutes later. He told me they were backdating my money because I was rehab. It worked out at £3800 approximately. Fuck me, I was well sorted. I didn't have a bank account so he sorted it out in giros. The maximum giro was for £449 so I had to go in Monday, Wednesday and Friday, to collect a giro for £449 until it had paid me back the £3800. When I went back to the Church that night, I told the boys that helped me to come to the off licence and pick their carry out of choice. Papa Smurf wanted 3 bottles of cheap cider. I told him to pick a whiskey, but no.

Papa Smurf was a legend. I was offering malt whiskey and he wanted cheap cider. The rest didn't hold back but I didn't give two shits. I bought a bit of weed for us all as well. We all lived well for a few days but the first £449 was away. I had though, found a room in a house and gotten my sister's boyfriend to pay the first month's rent. It was £400 for a room about 8ft x 10ft with a shitter and a shower in the corner. I had told the family that all was good. I was looking for work and going to AA, all bollocks. I was spending my days in the pub, some days with Papa Smurf and the guys. I always went back to see they were all good, buying the odd carry out. At night, I was going to a pub called fucking rehab. I went there because it was £1.50 a bottle of beer, a steal for London.

This set up went on about 3 months. I was back on the coke. My room was right outside Watford Junction. You could see the boys getting it sorted. They buzzed about on BMX and like wee ants. I got a number and if I wanted anything, it was there in 5-10 minutes. I was now spending most days in the pub at the end of the street, snorting then the money was getting low so I took to staying in my room drinking strong cans and bottles of wine or vodka. One night, I did venture out. It was late and the only place open was a gay club. So, fuck it, I was away in. They charge £10 for the privilege. I am total straight by the way so I must have stood out. A guy spotted me and heard the accent. He was Scottish. I told him "Mate, look, I am here for the drink". He said "I know mate, I can tell".

I had a great night at the gay bar but to be honest, I was fucked again. The drink had sneaked back in, the shakes were back. The landlord kept chasing me for rent and I kept him off my back by saying I was waiting to hear back from the social, blah blah, but he wasn't happy although he accepted it. I was down to my last £1000 and I wasn't parting with it for rent, no danger. I had still been bullshitting the family. My brother-in-law was still waiting for his £400 back. In fact, I think he is still waiting. He's a great guy though and was willing to help out. I had been in touch with my auntie and cousins in Coventry. My cousin was planning a visit for a while and one day she turned up out of the blue. I think she done it on purpose to try and catch me out as I had also been bullshitting them, saying all was good.

My cousin turned up. We had a night out and got hammered. She was shocked at the state I was in. You don't hand an alky just out of rehab £4000 nearly. I had been partying hard and it showed. We got back to my room and when I told her I was £400 in rent a month, she was even more shocked. She phoned my auntie and the decision was made. I was to come home to Coventry with her. We had a problem. My landlord stayed on the same street so if we were walking past with my suitcase, they would be out wanting rent. Me and my cousin watched for a full day, then at night, the landlord and his wife jumped into a taxi. As soon as the taxi was out of the street, we were off. Watford Junction was at the bottom of the street, so we didn't have far to run. I was off to Coventry. Me, my auntie and my cousin agreed to tell nobody. They didn't want my dad falling out with them.

Coventry, England (second time)

Coventry was the same old story. I was back to where I was before going into rehab. I was living on strong cider and vodka. My auntie thought I was only on the strong cider as I was sneaking the vodka. I helped with the shopping etc. but most of the time, I was sat on the couch drinking. My cousins smoked weed so there was always a joint on the go as well. I was fading away in front of my auntie's eyes; she later told me with tears in her eyes. She was lying to her brother and I was lying to the family, still making out I was in London. One day, my auntie sat me down and asked me to go home. She was scared she was going to find me dead on her sofa one day and how could she explain that to my mum and dad. I agreed to go home. My auntie said later when she was moving her furniture, about a dozen vodka bottles fell out the bottom. She could have easily found me dead.

Motherwell, Scotland

When I did get home, it was obvious to everyone I had been lying to them. I was obviously back on the drink. The constant shaking was a giveaway. They were all upset though and I felt like shite, but mum did not ever take a step backward. She promoted AA again, told me to get back to Chapel and get God in my life. I felt hopeless though. I couldn't see the point. The thought of drinking myself to death with some pills to help me along the way was becoming a viable option. It was only the fact my family still loved me that stopped me. How could they love me? I had everything going good for me, and look at me! I wasn't even 30. I had done 3 rehabs and failed. I couldn't brush my teeth without a strong can to stop me shaking. How the fuck could you love me? So, I wouldn't kill myself but I had no intention of stopping. It was too fucking hard.

Same old shit had to be done. I had to go homeless. If they had a bed, I got it, luckily or unluckily. I mean, I got a bed in a place in Motherwell called Airth Court. Same shit as Glasgow. Folks fighting over a can of beer or a roll up, and soon enough, I was in about it. I had made new drinking pals. There was always someone who got paid their benefit. So, we all took turns at feeding each other's drinking habits. The odd day we had to go stealing from Asda. I once got into a scrap with a guy who stole my tobacco. I was raging! Why steal from someone who is in the same situation? I couldn't get it and I battered him. The next day, he came to my flat with a bag of shopping to say sorry. The poor guy was desperate and too shy to ask. I told him to stop being shy or he wouldn't survive.

Newarthill, Scotland

There was a time my wee sister, when I was trying to get off the drink, took me in to try help me. It was her first wee flat with her husband (well at that time they weren't married but they are now). He is a brilliant guy; a genuine gentleman and I couldn't wish for a better guy for my sister. Well, it was their first flat they had together with their first son, so it was a lovely gesture on their part because I was really struggling. She was letting me have the odd can of lager to keep the demons away. At night, she was letting me user her computer to play poker on her husband's account. I thought it was for fun with kid on money. Well, it was her man's winnings I was playing with. Luckily, I had only lost £70 odd of his winnings. It was a mistake but he was amazing about it and not a cross word was said. He tried to make me not stress about it. I was feeling bad enough.

I had picked up a bit of hash saying it helped me while trying to wean myself off the drink. She wasn't on my case about it. Well, one day we were nipping out in the car and I was in the passenger seat. My sister holding her son, ready to put him in his car seat, when they next thing, armed police were all over the place. They let my sister run into the house with her son. I was told not to move. Next thing, 2 cars skidded up the pavement. One was full of police who dragged 2 guys and a girl out the car at gunpoint. Flat on their faces with a boot in their back. It turns out they had robbed a garage. My sister was thinking it was for me for a minute. A bit extreme for a bit of hash, but it's another example of love and kindness that was shown to me to help me get sober. It never worked this time but they tried and I won't forget that love ever.

Motherwell, Airth Court

When you lived in a place like Airth Court, there was a man for everything. Drugs, cheap tobacco, shoplifters that took orders and they very rarely failed! Anyway, there was a boy who would wire your electric meter for £10. Well, I got him to do mines. I watched him do it. He took the 16mm cooker wire, stripped it back about 2 inches until the copper was bare. He then slid it up the 2 outside black wires coming from the meter. Easy peasy I thought. He said it should last a couple of months and it did. But when it did, I thought, fuck giving him a tenner, I am giving this a go myself. I had watched him do it. Well fuck knows what I did but I blew myself from one end of the cupboard to the other and the meter was fucked. I had to go to the security office and report it. All the way down getting funny looks off everyone. I thought it was because of the bang it made.

When I went to the security hut, the guy had a right laugh when I told him all I had done was flick the switch behind my telly and bang. He told me to wait in the flat until the engineer came out. When he did, not long after he was laughing as well. I was saying to him some lousy bastard had rigged that meter. I am saying "the fucker could have killed me", playing all innocent that this fucked up, burnt out meter was nothing to do with me. All I done was flick a switch and all the while the engineer is saying "aye mate, some cunt has rigged this definitely". Well, when he left, I thought I would run a nice bath now that the electric was on, I could heat water. When I went into the bathroom, I caught a glimpse of myself in the mirror. My face was black like soot and my hair was singed. I think they all knew who the lousy bastard was.

I stayed there for months with not even an offer of a shed never mind a flat. I was about 3 miles from my family and my kids. I couldn't dare go near them in the state I was in. I was a mess. I actually cut my wrists one night, washed some paracetamols down with cheap cider and waited to go to sleep. The boy I battered over the tobacco came in and found me. The only person I would let him phone was my auntie in Coventry. She phoned my dad. If I had died and she knew, how could she live with herself. My dad turned up at the hostel, took me home, ran me a bath, made me a feed. We never mentioned the state of my wrists but again, another example of love. A kind act had saved me that day. I stayed a night, then disappeared back to Motherwell.

My dad's kind act was not enough. The draw of the drink was too much. I went back to the hell hole in Motherwell and carried on with my life drinking. In fact, it was no life, it was an existence. The most important thing in my existence was drink. Simple as that. I would have married a bottle of vodka. All I could think about was where my next drink was coming from. I took to sleeping with a can under my pillow, just so there was one for the morning. Once I had that, I could get to work on getting the rest that either meant spending my money, borrowing someone else's or stealing from Asda or Aldi. The one thing about alkies is they are resourceful. If we worked as hard at a business, it would be a success. There were days I couldn't get it and I was so ill those days, shakes, sweat and shivers etc.

One of the days when I woke up with nothing, I took a seizure. Luckily, an older guy who I was sharing with found me. This was a bad one. I was foaming at the mouth and the shaking went on for too long. He called an ambulance and I was hospitalized for 6 days. They detoxed me and my mum fought my case saying, now I was sober, I couldn't go back to the hostel as I would just start drinking again. She was right…I would have. I was absolutely choking for a drink. The social worker gave in and offered a scatter flat in a tower in Motherwell. This was a great result. A nice wee furnished flat. I got discharged and my mum got me in and settled. Me being me, had noticed the shop at the bottom of the flats. I talked mum into leaving me a tenner for the electric. She left and said she would be back with dinner. As soon as she was away, I was right down the shop for a half bottle and 2 cans. I got my arse back up before mum came back.

Mum got back with the dinner. I couldn't get rid of her quick enough. I had a half bottle to get tore into. Mum left. I got settled down in my room to watch the telly. I opened a can took a mouthful, turned the telly on and BOOM! The bastard went on fire. I woke up on the stairwell with a fireman trying to bring me round. I had been discharged from the hospital no more than 5 hours and I was in hospital fighting for my life after being pulled out of a fire by a neighbour I had never met. Luckily, I had not locked the door. I had left it on the latch so the boy next door booted the door in and dragged my sorry arse out. He even put a pair of trainers on me before being evacuated. The blocked was a high rise and I was number 10. They had to evacuate

2 floors above me. At hospital, my lungs were full of smoke and they were fighting to keep me breathing.

My cousin worked in the hospital. She wanted to call my mum but I begged her no to, but I was in such a bad way, they were worried I wouldn't make it. So, in the end my cousin called my mum. She said she couldn't live with it if I died and she hadn't got mum. In and out of consciousness, I can remember mum talking to the police. I found out later, they told her if I was over the drink limit, they would be charging me with fire raising. Mum told them to fuck off and that I was just detoxed. Luckily, I didn't get round to drinking my carry out. In the morning when I came round, I had a black face and the front of my t-shirt and jeans were melted. I had the guy who save my life's trainers on. I wanted to leave. There was a bit of a scene caused. The nurse wanted me to stay as I was still very ill. My lungs were full of smoke. In the end, they made me sign a book and I walked back to the flat. Even after all this, all I could think of, was drink.

I got back to the flat. It was taped off like a crime scene. The council workers were cleaning the white landing tiles. They knew by looking at me that it was me who was in the fire. I was black. They let me into the flat to see what I had left. The answer to that was, I had nothing. It was like walking through a bonfire. In a drawer in the kitchen, I found an AA book with a picture of my 2 kids. It was as if someone was trying to tell me something. On the way out, I managed to tap a tenner off the workers. I think they felt sorry for me. I was right down to the shop again. A half bottled and a couple of strong cans. I went down to sit at the Clyde, close to jumping and my phone went. My mum was back at the hospital. The doctors advised I came back. I agreed but only after I finished my drink. Mum picked me up with my brother and an AA guy.

All the way back to the hospital, my brother was trying to give me a talking to. Bad idea! I just laughed at him. As soon as the car got to the hospital, we all got out and I walked round and lamped my brother (square go at the hospital take 2). Me and him again, rolling around like 5-year-olds. My poor mum, in the middle of it, tights all ripped trying to split us up. In the end, some boys out for a fag chased my brother away. I got wheeled into the hospital. This time, it was the police who turned up. They asked me If I wanted my brother charged. "What for?" I asked, "it was me who punched him first" then laughed. My mums screaming in the background, "charge both the bastards, I will get peace!" The poor woman was shattered. I got another few days in the hospital, lucky again.

After the fire, the family, aunts, uncles, etc., all chipped in to get me kitted out with clothes because, literally, I had fuck all. `I never ever met the neighbour. I did hand in his trainers and a bottle. If the family hadn't done what they did, I would have had nothing. How did I show my appreciation? The new hostel called the Blue Triangle was full of boys I knew and it wasn't long before I was back on the drink. I also bumped into a guy who I knew from Newarthill, who I actually had a run in with earlier in life. Well, drink brought us together and we became great pals. In fact, he is the guy who played a big big part in me getting sober. He was an Army Vet with PTSD. He had a nice wee home. For weeks, I spent a lot of time with him there.

Mossend, Scotland

North Lanarkshire Council must have been shitting it in case I sued them for the fire because they came up with an offer of a flat for me. A 2-bedroom flat maisonette. Mossend is about 2 miles from Newarthill. My sister came with me to view the flat. There was a pub one corner and an off license on the other. Perfect for an alky. My sister said "bad move don't you think?" I didn't give a shit. I had been homeless on and off for long enough. I was taking it no matter what. I moved in, done up the living room and half a kitchen, then chucked a bed in the room. I was pretty chuffed with myself and settled down for a drink. On the way back, I met one of the neighbours and invited him and another couple up for a drink. Again, I made pals, same as everywhere else.

Me and my new drinking buddies were all getting on great. Just like me, they were all alkies. We would gather in one guy in particulars flat all the time as his flat was closer to the shop and on the ground floor. We all helped each other out when stuck, as I have said before, most alcoholics have a good heart. My mate, the Army Vet, was still a regular visitor, thank fuck. He always had a drink on him. His PTSD scared the others though, but I knew how to calm him and I had a number for a guy who ran a Veteran's Centre. I called him one day as my pal had really lost it. The guy from the Centre said to bring him down to him. So, we put him in a taxi and as we waited, the police turned up and took my mate away to be sectioned. He was sat in the police car with a can in his hand. The police were afraid to take it off him. The guy from the Centre said it was for his safety.

When I got back to Mossend from the Veteran Centre, the guys were all relieved that my mate had been sectioned as the way he was acting was really freaking them out. So, just they breathed a sigh of relief, my mate walked in. he had escaped from the secure hospital and they wouldn't come to Mossend as that had not took our addresses. So, they would have been looking in Motherwell. I was glad to have him around. He was a good pal although we were all drinkers, he would always get in my ear saying my mum was right, that I was still young enough to get sober. Bullshit I said as I'd already tried rehab 3 times and I was living proof they didn't work. He said I had just ended up in the wrong types of rehabs. The ones before we businesses. He kept telling me about one in Dundee that was run by alcoholics. A non-profit thing and they were only in it to help other alkies. I filed that to the back of my head.

Mossend was the same as everywhere else I ended up. The maisonettes were 2-bedroom flats on the first landing with the 1-bedroom flats on the bottom. Next door to me was a mother and daughter. The mum was an alcoholic. The daughter looked after the mum and to be fair, they tried looking after me, handing in grub, the odd can and always good for a bit tobacco. Along was a guy around 40 years old. He was alcoholic, then on the bottom flats, there were another 3 guys, all alcoholics. I was an excellent shoplifter and always sorted out some food for us, sometimes clothes. One Christmas, Aldi were selling winter jackets, but they were red. We were all walking around like the mountain rescue but we didn't care! More money for drink. We always sat in 1 flat on the ground floor.

We had not a bad system. We all got our benefits on different days so someone always had a carry out. My mum and dad would visit to make sure I was still alive, usually on a Sunday with a pot of home-made soup. That's what kept me alive some weeks. I done up the living room of my house and nothing else. I was only interested in drink. One Sunday, we were sitting in the usual guys flat. We all had a good drink in us and we noticed the guy on the same landing had not been seen for a couple of days. The last time I saw him was Friday when he chapped my door to ask for a roll up. So, we all went up to see him. His flat was in darkness and his dog going mental. We found him dead. When we rolled him over, this was in his toilet, half his face was missing. We could see his eye socket.

The poor guy had gone to the toilet and collapsed. He once told me when he was lying drunk that his dog, called Marley, would lick his face to wake him up. The police think that he had cut his face when he fell again the artex wall and his dog began licking his face to wake him up. They think it got a taste for blood and because it was hungry, it began eating at him. The police kept us in the one flat as the guys flat was a crime scene. His brother turned up in the middle of it all and 3 of us had to hold him down to stop him getting into his brothers flat. Nobody had to see what we had. The police even let us send out for more drink and they let us have a joint. We were all in severe fucking shock. My mum also appeared.

The police let me out to speak to my mum. She was bawling her eyes out as she really thought it was me this time. She told me in no uncertain terms that if I didn't get my shit together, it was me next. And again, she was spot on. The guy had died with pneumonia. His dog had to be put down as they said it now had a taste for blood. Mum was right. The way I was living, it could soon be me. After the guy's funeral, I pulled my mate who mentioned the rehab to me to one side. I wanted to go give it a go again. I was shitting myself that I was going to be found behind my door one day. My health was terrible. I couldn't hold food down; my eyes were constantly streaming. I hadn't had a solid shit for ages. It was definitely time to go for it.

My mate got the ball rolling. The rehab was in Dundee. A house where each man had their own 1 bed flat. The deal was, I had to go to Dundee every second Thursday to go to an AA meeting and meet the rest of the guys. I done it. My mate had a bus pass. I was his project. No matter what state I was in, he made sure my sorry arse was on that bus. I done this a few times until one day, a phone call came. A flat was available. I didn't even empty my Mossend flat. I left it open and told the guys to help themselves to what furniture was there. I had moved in with mum and dad as the plan was, they were dropping me off on their way to a cottage in Aberfeldy they had booked with my aunts and my sister. I had other ideas…one last party!

Aberfeldy, Scotland

Dad and my sister had been sent ahead to the cottage in Aberfeldy. Mum and an aunt were staying with me to drop me at the rehab in Dundee. I ended up wrecked and threatening no to go. I can admit now that this was nothing else but total fear. I knew what was coming and it scared me. I had done it plenty times before, so mum, to be sure I got to Dundee, decided to con me into getting into the car and took me to Aberfeldy, that was closer to Dundee. When we got there, my dad, uncles, sister etc., were all sat there like altar boys, not a drink in the house. They had stashed all the drink. I called them all the bastards under the sun. I went to bed raging. They had put all the drink in the car boots. I heard them all sneaking out for it when they thought I was asleep.

When I got up in the morning, I was shaking. My uncle chucked a can my way to stop the shakes. I think they were scared in case I done a runner. My dad was looking out the window calling my 2 auntie's dogs disgusting. They were trying to hump each other. Both were boys but I think he was trying to create a better atmosphere. They eventually got me in the car to Dundee. I said a teary cheerio to them all. They loved me that much, they actually fucking kidnapped me to make sure I got to the rehab, and one of the boys who ran it met me at the door. Dad handed him £50 to cover my first week. That was the last time I seen or heard from any of the family for 3 months.

Dundee, Scotland

The Dundee rehab was bang in Central Dundee. A pub at the corner and on the drive in, I must have counted a dozen within a couple of miles. How the alcoholic head works. I was pub counting and I hadn't even booked into the rehab. Mum and dad were away. The full family must have breathed a sigh of relief. The rehab was a house owned by Monks, donated to help alkies. It was run by 2 men both in recovery. For years, there were other staff members and they were all alcoholics in recovery as well. There was a cook, a lovely woman who never touched a drink in her life. She had worked there for 10+ years. I had my own flat. There was a house meeting in the morning then you were expected to go to AA meetings a minimum of 5 per week. I was introduced to the guys, all the same as me, all at different staged. I was given a mate who never left my side. He sat with me through my rattle, ate with me, the lot.

I had a door key and I could come and go as I pleased up until 11 pm. The first 3 weeks, I had to have someone with me to go to the shop, meeting etc. Each day, I had to walk past the pubs to go to AA. It was fucking torture that first few weeks. The mate I had, talked me round a few times. I wanted to drink so much it. It was a great bunch and, in a way, each and every one of them helped keep me there. I worked with one of the staff going through the big book of AA. I questioned it all. The sponsor was from the Isle of Barra. He told me as much about him as I told him about me. My routine was 2 meetings a day and a session with my sponsor. I even started going back to Chapel. I got God back into my head. I done everything that was suggested. I knew if I didn't get this, I was going back out to die, simple!

As the weeks passed, it got easier and easier to walk past the pubs, not wanting to go in. That feeling to have to go in and get a drink was leaving me. It felt good walking past them. It was like some sick test I put myself through, and sick is a good word. I started to understand I was sick in the head and in the body. When I put drink in me, that was it, the control was gone. I had to have more; my body demanded it. I was sick in the head because come on, who the fuck would want to live the life I have been living if they didn't have a sickness in the head? Three months had passed and I spoke to my family. They had been calling to check I was still there but the manager advised them not to talk to me, to leave me to concentrate on myself. This was a clever man.

I had made some great pals. I swear today that it's the correct people in your life at the right time that will help you get sober. I was lucky I had the perfect combination. They guys saved my life, that's the truth. My mum brought my kids to visit me, the first time in ages I had seen them. Then, I got to take my son and nephew to a Celtic vs Dundee United game, and for my sister to trust me with the most precious thing in her life, was a statement of how well I was doing and that the trust was coming back. A small thing to many was massive to me. The good things that I was being promised in the AA rooms, were starting to happen. Fuck me! I hadn't been lied to. I used to sit and listed saying "pish" under my breath. At one meeting, a boy I got talking to, found out I was a joiner and offered me work.

I spoke to my sponsor and he thought the job was a great idea. So, I took it but it was what I was used to. It was in an industrial estate, keeping it tidy. I was really starting from the bottom now; I was a fucking janny/litter picker. I spent the day walking around picking up used condoms, needles, nappies. You fucking name it, I picked it up for £40 a day, but fuck it, the only way is up now. In the rehab, if you slipped, and some guys did, they didn't kick you out. They put you up in a hotel for 2 weeks and gave you the chance to get back on track. If this did happen, we would all rally round. I didn't slip but a couple of guys did and we always managed to get them back on track. One guy had been jumping out his window going to a nightclub every night and we never had a clue. Fly as fuck, alkies.

I met all sorts in there. A guy I am still pals with today, had been jailed for tying his brother-in-law up and pouring petrol over him because of a drug debt. It was him that owed the debt! I also sat with a Priest one night. He told me the Church put all the troublesome Priests in a house in the middle of nowhere to repent. Well, he never repented, he got worse! So, the next place for him was rehab, the next after that, was out of Priesthood. He told me he got stopped by a Traffic Policeman one night. He was well over the limit and he knew the Police Officer as he had done his wedding for him. So, when the Officer told him he was getting charged, the Priest piped up and said, "you wee bastard, I never charged you for your wedding!" My point? Different people, different ages, all talking and all caring for each other.

I had started getting sore feet. So, when I got them x-rayed, I was told I would need surgery on my feet to straighten them out. My toes were all bent. Probably from an injury I never dealt with because it would have interrupted my drinking. It had caught up with me now. I had also been talked into internet dating. I never had a clue so I got help from one of the boys to set it up. Thank fuck because I found my new wife. I started talking to a cracking lassie from Fife but I had a predicament. Do I be honest? Now this was a gamble. Do I tell her everything and give her the chance to run like fuck or do I lie and then, look a prick when the truth comes out? Up to now, since I got to Dundee, the honesty thing was working pretty well. So, fuck it! I was honest.

When I started talking to my now wife on the phone, it cost us a lot of sleep. Some nights we sat up talking until 3 in the morning. We were also running up a big phone bill. She had a son, so meeting was going to be put off until he had been away. But, after talking for ages, telling her everything, I was desperate to meet her. Fucks sake, I had told this girl everything about me, all the shite I had been through, the baggage I came with. Well, she was still interested. I soon discovered she has the biggest heart in a person I've ever known. Beautiful inside and out. One weekend, my now stepson was at his dads. We took the chance to get together. I told her I would tell her after 5 minutes if I wanted to be with her. I knew after 2 seconds. She was stunning! Another good thing coming my way. The AA stuff was coming true big time.

I was now coming up on 8 months sober. I had my wee job which was now really important, as I needed bus fare to Fife. I had found my future wife. Next, was a flat and I got a wee cracker at the top of the biggest hill in Dundee. Not the best idea as the foot surgery was fast approaching. I got the flat looking great. Things just kept coming my way. People donated furniture etc. People helped me move, my now wife helped, my mum came up and they both went shopping. All the boys jumped into action and helped. The day came to get my surgery. They done both feet at once. Between my future wife and my best mate, I was well looked after. He was up every morning with my paper and fags and my wife would take my now step son to school and then come to Dundee to give me haircuts and feed me.

When I first went to meet my new wife, my mate said "you will end up moving". He was spot on. My flat was great and my stepson began coming with his mum to stay. The flat had a room in the basement, so he loved sitting down there most of the time with my mate. I wasn't into Playstations like they were. The room had a shower which I used to sit in to get a shower. I had a piss bucket next to the bed to save me struggling through the night. My wife ended up nearly covered in it one morning. Another time, I was constipated because of pain relief, well, she was brushing her teeth and

I had to burst in to sit on the pan. She was already having to put up with a lot so it was time for me to move on again. This time, it was a flitting to Fife. Me and my mate done it on an all-day bus ticket.

Fife, Scotland

When I started going back and forth to Fife to spend time with my wife to be, I also got to know her son better. He was an easy wee guy to fall in love with and to this day, he is a strapping 22-year-old and I can honestly say, I have never had a harsh word. I am honoured and lucky to have him in my life. I began going on a Friday. The weekends turned into long weekends and eventually, I moved full time. I kept my flat going as long as I could as there were some of the boys struggling. And if they had a slip up, I let them use my flat to get their shit together. My wife to be stayed in a flat that was 3 flights up, and as I had 2 broken feet, it was a bit of a struggle but I was happy to be there. I had found a great woman and we were totally in love with the added bonus of my stepson and my wife's family were amazing. I had hit the jackpot.

The part of Fife, Leven, was a beautiful place, lovely beaches. If you went left or right, you would land on a beach. I had begun to get my kids up for weekends. I had got over my surgery and wife's uncle, who had a small building company, gave me a start working with him. To this day I will be ever grateful to him. He took a chance and he didn't know me from Adam. He must have known I was just out of rehab and he must have been shitting himself, but we hit it off great, and to this day, I have a great relationship with him and his wife, my wife's auntie. All was going great and it was to get even better. We found out we had a baby on the way. The whole family were buzzing, both sides, but there was a bit of a dampener put on it when I got a letter from my kids' mum from back in Motherwell. It was from a Lawyer and she was asking me to walk away from my kids.

I guess everyone wasn't as happy as we all were, but how could I walk away? My wife was adamant we had to put up a fight. She had wished her own son's dad had fought for him. So, I had to find a Lawyer, which I did, and the fight was on. For the court case, I had to travel to Hamilton Sherriff Court. I had 3-4 appearances and I had to sit and listen to a load of lies and keep cool. My wife kept drilling into me that this wasn't about me, that this was for the kids. I felt invincible though, with this woman at my side, I could do anything. So, I sat in silence with a smile and left my Lawyer to do my talking. I got the feeling the Judge was warming to me when he said to the other Lawyer, after a statement was read out by the family of the kids' mum, running me down and telling everyone about the terrible things I had done, the Judge turned and said I don't do that now.

I was right! The Judge was warming and he granted me access. But, to begin with, access was from my mother's home. By this time, we had a new baby boy, but without fail, we managed. Sometimes, travelling on a Friday on the train with a new baby and my step son but we done it Friday – Sunday for as long as was needed. My wife backed me all the way as she had fell in love with my kids before all this court crap had started. My step son had begun building relationships with them as well, so every 2nd weekend, we done the journey with no complaints. The very first weekend this arrangement started, my past was to come bit me on the arse and it was a total set up to get me a kicking. I had my suspicions. Only one other party knew the arrangement. We were all heading out for the day, me, my wife, stepson, new baby son, mum and dad, my sister and her kids. My dealer from back in the day, the guy I worked in Buxton and Ayrshire with, turned up and told me to get into his car. I quickly told the family not to worry. My sister knew this guy and his reputation. I was due him around £1000 for a coke bill from years ago. I got in the car with him. I found out later, everyone in my mum's was frantic.

My sister took the registration of the car in case I didn't come back. I was back within half an hour. Whoever had set me up for a kicking, well the plan had backfired. This guy was still scary but he was now having his own struggles with drink and was more interested in asking me what he could do to get his life back on track. I advised him best I could and gave him my number. I told him to call me to talk anytime he wanted. This was all lovely but he still wanted his money.

He told me who had told him that I would be at my mum's every 2nd weekend. I was raging. This was the same person who had been messaging my wife when she was pregnant, telling her I would leave her with a kid blah, I was a bastard blah blah, but my honesty at the start of our relationship paid off. There was nothing that could be said in court that I hadn't told my wife, so bring it on! I had come to an arrangement with the guy to give him what I could every 2nd weekend. He actually wanted me to work with him again to work it off but my sister and the rest didn't want me going back down that road again. They just wanted this guy out of my life. So, she got me a loan so I could pay him off, which I did on the 2nd weekend visit. He said I will get your name out the "book". I had been on a kicking list for years.

All was good. This guy got paid, we were getting on with things, doing my visits every 2nd weekend. Things were great. I was a new dad, I had an amazing new partner who to this day, amazes me at how much of a caring, loving person she is. Every 2nd week, she made sure we made our visits, never let anyone down and it paid off. The supervised visits at my mum's were to stop and I was able to have my full family with me in Fife for visits. Brilliant! We needed more room, and after a while, moved across the road from the flat. I had stopped working with my wife's uncle and started working with my brother in laws father, fitting out kitchen showrooms. It was all over the country. It meant leaving my new family, but the money was great so I couldn't knock it back.

This new job, and I can say this with confidence, was the best job I ever had. The boy I worked for was a gem of a guy and I still call him a pal today. We sometimes go on holiday together with the rest of my wife's family. This guy would not have his workers living in conditions that he wouldn't himself, so the digs and grub were always top notch. Swimming pools in the hotel etc. The first week, I think I had a steak every night, the boys had a few beers but I wasn't interested, a fucking miracle. For a guy who used to put a can of strong cider under his pillow and would have married a bottle of vodka. I did miss everyone, but the boys were all like a big family. In fact, we were all related through marriage. We would get flown home to get back to our families quicker. I now also had a niece and nephew from my wife's sisters and I loved them all.

Things were brilliant. I had my new family in Fife. A lovely wife and step son. Regular access with my other 2 kids. Mum and dad were at peace now. I was finally getting my shit sorted. I was seeing my sister and her 2 kids. She now had a new baby daughter, plus, the family in Fife was growing. Then, bang! One Christmas we were off for a couple of weeks. I began getting pain in my back and legs. I put it down to stiffness as we had been working long hard hours, so I just thought my body was seizing up because we had stopped. By the time it came to go back, I was in agony. I went to the doctor, was given pain relief and referred for a scan. This went on for months. I tried for months to carry on but in the end, I was really struggling and had to give the job fitting kitchen showrooms up. It was just getting too hard.

I was gutted leaving that job. It took months to get some sort of benefits sorted out so money was becoming a struggle. I started doing shifts with my wife's uncle again but some mornings I was in tears with pain going to work. My wife said enough was enough. I was ending up in A&E as I still had no word of the scans requested by my doctor. After one visit to A&E, the on-call doctor ordered a scan. By this time, taking a step was leaving me in agony, like an electric shock going up my leg, into my arse cheek and up my arm into my neck. When the scans came back, there was a number of discs at the top and bottom of my back which were compressing my nerves. I was told I would need surgery again and that the nerve damage would be permanent. Fucking Brilliant! A year or so ago, I would have run for a drink, but not this time.

I got taken into Ninewells hospital for the surgery on my back. When that was done, they broke it to me that the discs at the top of my back were too dangerous to operate on, and the risks outweighed the benefits. I was being sent to Glasgow Royal for surgery to remove 2 extra bones that were compressing my nerves in my neck. This was rare and was the reason for the arm pain. The surgery was in Glasgow as it could only be done by a professor there since it was so delicate and rare. My wife had just passed her driving test and had never drove to Glasgow, but she did it with no complaints. All of this was affecting her as well and our young family but not once did she moan or make me feel worse. She was only concerned about me. It was actually her who talked me into stopping working for my own good. She didn't give a shit about the money.

My wife is a different breed of woman, and I regularly tell her this. She had taken me on, firstly after hearing my back story, I was in a rehab, so had nothing material to offer her. Then I dragged her through a court case, surgery on my feet and now surgery on my back. You couldn't grudge her having a moan but she never did and never has. After the back surgery, I stayed mainly in the bedroom upstairs as the toilet was there. We put in for a move but in the end, we had to find a private let. I still had the neck surgery to come so I needed a room and toilet downstairs. The house was only 2 bedrooms so was getting crowded. We moved into a lovely wee cottage. We loved it there and it had everything we needed, rooms for all the kids and a toilet and bedroom downstairs. It was ideal and to add to the fact, my wife was pregnant again.

We were expecting again! This was great news and we were buzzing. But, in the back of my head, I still knew the neck surgery was coming. When they explained to me who dangerous the operation was and the risks involved, I had my wife and mum in the room. I turned round to ask how they felt about it and they were both sitting crying. Nothing like setting your mind at ease. The bottom line was, it needed done. The plan was one side then 3 months later, the other side. I got the surgery done and survived but the damage was done. I was diagnosed with chronic regional pain syndrome and have been left in daily pain. I will be on pain relief for the rest of my days and I now use a stick to get around. However, I was still a happy boy. I still thought myself a lucky boy. I had a new wife to be, a new stepson, my others kids in my life and my family back.

You probably think I am off my nut. How the fuck am I lucky? Well, out of the 10 boys I was in rehab with in Dundee, there were only 4 of us left. My wee pal who had helped keep me in rehab and helped after my surgery, the boy who was going to set his brother-in-law on fire, another guy who went back to Airdrie to be with his family, and then me. I was lucky and I knew it. I got the surgery done on my neck, again, my wife to be, my wee pal and my family supported me throughout. But Fife Council had other ideas. We had been in the cottage for over a year and they were stopping paying full benefit for the rent. They were making us homeless. They wanted to split us up in hostels. I had lived that life and no way was I dragging my new family through that shit.

We now had another new baby, a girl. So, there was me, my wife to be, my stepson, our son and now a new baby girl. The council came up with a scatter flat in Methil, the next village to Leven. It was fucking bogging so the first thing we done was get a cleaning firm in to shampoo all the carpets. By now, my wife to be had trained in home care. She was now our main bread winner. We kept on at the council and in the end, after a few months in the shithole scatter flat, they offered us a ground floor flat, 4 in a block. This is the house we now live in. They put in a shower room to make my life easier. We live there with my stepson who is now 22 years old, our son who is now 11 years old and our daughter who is 7 years old. My son from Motherwell, is now 18 years old and my eldest daughter is 23 years old. Unfortunately, she doesn't speak to us anymore as there was a fall out over court.

So, just to bring you up to date, I now live in Fife, Methil in fact, with my wife to be, my 22-year-old stepson, our son 11 and our daughter 7. My 18-year-old son is still in our lives but my daughter who is 23, had her head turned by all the court stuff She was also told a lot of lies. It is sad but I choose now to concentrate on what I had got and not what I have lost.

I keep calling my wife to be, my wife to be because we only managed to get married in July 2022. We had gotten engaged in 2012 but the first date, we had to move because of all my surgery, the other 2 dates had to be moved during Covid and eventually we managed to get married on July 30th 2022. I spent most of the day bubbling, and to be fair, so did everyone else. I think everyone couldn't believe the day had come. During dad's speech, he said it all, through tears though. He said "Liam is the happiest I have ever seen him". Never a truer word said. Look what I have in my life? A new wife, my stepson, my son and daughter and a relationship with my other son who I thought I would lose. I have the rest of my family all back in my life and they were all at the wedding. I had 3 best men, all of my sons. I was the proudest guy alive.

I am now back working. I trained to do a home-based job doing customer services, answering phones for IKEA. I had never used a computer since high school. I am not any sort of whizz kid but I know enough to do the job and get a wage, another thing I thought I had lost. It's a shitty wage but it's still a wage. My wife still does homecare and now plans going into the hospitals to work. She is well suited to this line of work. She has the biggest heart in anyone I ever know. Such a big heart, that when in Dundee, she actually came to AA to find out all about the alcoholics. She became good pals with all my mates. My one good pal from the rehab sadly lost his battles 2 years ago. I was in training when my wife found out the news. She tried to keep it from me to let me finish training but her face said it all and she had to tell me. I kept on going with the training as he would have wanted me to carry on. In the end, it was street valium that had killed him. He had only come to visit 2 weeks earlier, and looking back, I can now see how much he was struggling. It's only me and 1 other guy, the guy who poured petrol on the brother-in-law. He is still drinking, so I fear it will only be a matter of time before his body gives in and I get that dreaded phone call.

Just to recap, now I am coming up on 13 years sober. I have a beautiful new wife after 4 attempts to get that ring on her finger. I have a beautiful stepson who, when we first told him his mum was pregnant the first time with his wee brother, he lifted his head and looked at me and asked how I managed to do that with 2 broken feet. Fucking brilliant! I now have a cracking son who is 10 and a beautiful princess of a daughter aged 7. I have a great relationship with my 18-year-old son but still estranged with my 23-year-old daughter. I work in a wee office under the stairs, answering calls for IKEA. My wife is a home carer and now waiting to start work in the local hospital. My stepson works for the company I did, doing kitchen showrooms. He loves it and my 18-year-old son is training to be a painter and decorator.

Sober for nearly 13 years, I have now documented my life and how I got there. I haven't mentioned any names to protect people's anonymity, which is very important. There is no set way of getting sober. If there was, it would be too fucking easy. Everyone's journey is different. I had 4 rehabs and only 1 wasn't a business. The businesses failed for me. Not to say that's the case for everyone. I think when I got to the Dundee rehab, everything was lined up for it to be a success. This time, the correct bunch of guys, the managers and staff were alcoholics, so that helped. Even though right in Dundee City Centre, they gave us a key to the door, telling me that only I could sort myself out. It gave me responsibility of getting myself to meetings etc. They would be there to help and guide me but they weren't going to hold my hand.

I had to change the people and company I kept. As I said, I have only 3 pals still in my life from back in the day and they have had my back from day 1. When I left rehab, I was lucky with meeting my wife, who has also had my back from day 1. When she agreed to marry me, my sister asked if she was "aff her nut!" My stepson and my other kids have given me a purpose so the right people have to be in your life. People who make you want to do it. They don't know how much they help me without doing anything in particular. Just being there and loving me seems to be enough. My extended family help as well. I now have a load of nieces and nephews who I totally adore. I have my wee job that makes me feel useful. Alkies need to feel needed. Its in our DNA. I try to help others that are suffering. Sometimes I am successful, sometimes I'm not.

I wanted to write about my journey. Firstly, for my mum to see it before she is too ill to remember it. She is now getting on and her health isn't good. I wanted to show all the family and friends who supported me that I am grateful. But our main reason was, to show other alcoholics and addicts that there isn't a set way to get sober, that there are many ways. There are rehabs, councilors, 12 step programmes...if one works for you, then brilliant. But I have found I needed a bit of everything. I needed AA and even the shitty rehabs, I learned something. I had time with councilors who got me to start talking. When doing this, I realised how ill I was and that as soon as I put drink into me, that was the most important thing to me. Not even the love of a good family could keep me off the drink and trust me, they tried.

Conclusion

Drink and drugs are a bastard. They will take everything. It took a healthy young man with a trade and a good prospect and turned him into a homeless shoplifting alcoholic whose family couldn't have him in their home. That's how it was for me but I believe certain people were put in my life to guide me in the right way and to the right people. That's what happened with my mate who got me to Dundee. When I got there, I was with people the same as me, not therapists who had learned from a book. You can't learn about alcoholism from a book, you need to have lived it to be taken seriously. Even the other boys in there were perfect for what I needed. When I left and met my wife, she also turned out to be what I needed. Was it God or luck I met these people? I don't care…I am only grateful.

All the boy in Dundee, dead and alive, they all did their bit as well. Especially "G" who saved me many days. I wish the poor guy could have saved himself as well. So, thank you to everyone above. You all played massive parts in my journey.

To anyone still suffering, don't give up. Find that person, place, church, doctor, whatever the help you need, it's out there. If you work as hard at finding that person or place as you do finding the first can of the day, you will be OK. It needs a big effort from you as sobriety needs to be found. It won't chap on your door so keep trying. There are many different ways but the 2 main ingredients are the right place and the right people. Although I haven't put names to places, if you reach out, I will help you. So, here's to staying sober!

Now happily married, father of 5, I wanted to do this to show others it can be done. If one place doesn't work, find another plan. Don't give up, keep looking for that way out because when you do it, it's amazing. I suffer pain on a daily basis but it's nothing compared to the pain I was in mentally and physically when still on the drink. It's hard work just finding that first drink to set you up for the day, only to be fit enough to find more to take you to the oblivion every alky is after. I usually found that oblivion was better than the pain people are in, but if you can avoid that first one, you have half a chance. If you can avoid the first one, seek an AA meeting. You may get lucky like me and find the person the same as you that can help you.

Although I have written this anonymously, if anyone needs to know the places I am talking about, reach out by email. I will be glad to pass on any information they need, to seek help. So finally, to make it simple to get sober, the place has to be right, the people have to be right, but most importantly, the person has to want it. If it seems hopeless, read this because there is hope anyone can do it if I can. Reach out if needed. I won't ignore you.

I want to give some folks a special mention as they deserve it. Firstly, my wife! If I hadn't met her, I don't know how I would be. The things she has given me, 3 wonderful kids, unwavering support and encouragement when I need it. She is a wonderful person with a beautiful heart. I am lucky to call her my wife and my kids are lucky to call her their mum. I want to thank my parents who were there for me in the good and the bad times, and anytime I wanted to try, they had my back. They had to go through all the fuck ups, hospitals, you name it, I put them through it. And now, I am being serious about being a dad. I now realise how hard it was to watch me destroy and kill myself. I want to thank my sister and brother-in-law who also backed me when I was trying. My wee brother who put up with a lot as well, especially the "square goes!" My extended family in Fife, all my new nieces and nephews who have all showed me love, that I appreciate and I love them all as well. All the places, therapists, doctors etc., even if they didn't help at that particular time, they still helped. I want to say thanks to TQ, WA and FM who all stood by me and showed me true friendship and love.

To finish up, don't get me wrong, getting sober is the hardest thing I have ever done, but everyday I woke up rattling like an old Lada. I always managed to get a drink. I work hard every day to get a drink. One day, I walked about 3 miles because I had thrown a bag of cans into a bush to hide them from the police. That's dedication! So, I became dedicated to getting sober. At the start, I hammered AA because that's the only place I felt safe and normal, in with my own people. I had to change the people I kept in my life and today, I have 3 close pals who have always been there for me. They wanted nothing in return, only to have their old pal back and I want to thank them. They know who they are. These are the ones who came to visit me homeless, take me for a feed and put money in my pocket, knowing I would probably spend it on drink. But it stopped me risking jail or a kicking by stealing or shoplifting.

I had to change the places I went. I only go back to Newarthill to visit my parents, siblings or pals but I try not to socialize there unless it's a family meal. I stay safe. "If you keep going to the barbers, one day you will get a haircut". Although, I am now OK with going into a pub, restaurant or party without the drink bothering me, it took ages to feel comfy. At the start, if someone had sprayed anti-freeze on their windscreen, it made me think of drink, so now I stay safe. People still ask if it's ok to have a drink, especially my dad. I always reply of course, it's my problem, nobody else's Why should my presence waste everyone else's fun? That's not fair. If these situations were causing me to think of drinking, I would just walk out. No fuss, just quietly leave. Luckily up 'til today, it doesn't bother me. Just the other night, my wife, my stepson and his girlfriend were having a drink at the house. There was a load of drink sitting in the kitchen and my stepson came in and asked me if I wanted all the booze put out of the way. I said no because, in a sick way, I get a wee buzz knowing its there and I don't want it. That's a fucking miracle in itself as I would have married a bottle of buckfast.

Talking of marriage, luckily, I didn't marry a bottle of buckfast. Instead, I married the most beautiful person inside and out. This girl took a big risk on me. I had been honest from day 1 so she knew what I was, but she went and educated herself. She went to AA to sit with a room of strange men just so she knew what illness I had. They all loved her as she didn't judge them or look down on them when they shared their stories. Since then, she was 100% in. She was also taking a risk with my stepson as she had kicked his dad to the kerb for similar behaviour. Every operation I have had, she was there when I woke up and she's nursed me back to health each time. When it came to fighting for my other 2 kids, she kept me going when it got tough and now with my son in particular as she never got the chance with my daughter, but with him, she became as good a mum as she is amazing with him as she is with the other children. I think he talks to her more than me and they have a great laugh. He loves her too, I can see it clearly and it makes me so proud of her, so I want to thank her for the wonderful gift of being a dad again. I thought I would never experience that unconditional love, so thank you my wonderful wife. You don't realise what you do for me and I love you.

I also want to say a few words about my kids. The 2 older boys are turning into fine young men, pursuing different trades and making a right good go of their lives. I am so proud of you both. Thank you for giving me the chance to be your dad. I will try my hardest to be there for you and support you. The youngest 2 are also turning into fine wee humans who give me joy every day. Luckily, you have only seen me sober and I will try to keep it that way. And finally, mum, dad, my sister and brother who could have given up on me a long time ago but they never gave up on me. So, thank you! I love you all loads.

To anyone still suffering, who has lost everything, don't give up hope. There are ways out. If you keep trying, good things can happen. Everything I have lost. Getting sober brought it all back so it can happen for you. Remember the two P's, People and Places. Change them and you will change and that's the start.

Here today and gone tomorrow

Everything I have today has taken me a long time to get but in one drink to my lips, that's it gone, all lost again. Firstly, my good wife would not put up with it and second, the drink would win. It always does! I wish I could drink the way it should be done, to have fun, to be social and make pals. I can't do that with drink, it's oblivion or nothing. That's where it ends, with me on my arse with nothing. I love what I have today and I don't want to lose it. It's amazing. Everyday I see my kids and put them to bed. This year, we are going on our first holiday abroad, and this mad alky is going all inclusive. But, if I start wanting drink, I will be on the first plane home. That's how important it is to me to stay away from the drink. I am a lucky lucky man today.

The last page

"Thank fuck" you will all be thinking, but I can't finish without sending a message to anyone suffering. Anyone scratching about for the price of a can or a bag or a punt. Alkies, addicts, gamblers, we are all the same. We are ill. Of course we are! Who in their right mind would want to live the lives we lead? If you are feeling hopeless, then don't. There is a way out, not one that's easy. It involves pain, withdrawals, facing the horrors of what you have put folks through, everything you have lost. If you keep trying, you will find a path, a way out. Just keep looking. Everything I lost; I have gotten back ten-fold. In fact, thousands folds! Not financially but in my head, peace of mind, no anxiety, feeling emotions, all that comes back.

As you have read, drink and drugs took a lot from me, mentally and physically. But today, I consider myself a very rich man. Not materialistically, fuck I am rooked, I couldn't even afford to publish this book fucks sake, but I am lucky. My health is shite but I can still do my wee job and between me and my beautiful wife, we get by. The kids get all they need. I get to see my kids first thing in the morning and I tuck them in at night, Hollie sometimes a few times as she kicks her covers off. The older ones, I have to make an appointment as they are always up to something. I have a great relationship with my parents. They are at ease with me now. My siblings, I have back in my life and even my aunts and uncles can put up with me.

I have a great bunch of in laws who I love to bits. After reading this, they might not like me much!! I am only kidding! They knew I am an alky. I was honest so have to hide nothing. I have a wonderful wife who I wish I had met years ago. Its because of her that I have what I have. She made sure I have reasons to stay sober. All of this stuff is priceless and I got it all back. It all started with that last bender before Dundee. After that, I put it down, started talking it through with people like me. At first, loads of meetings, but it started there. So, again, anyone still suffering in pain, don't give up, don't stop trying. There is always a way if you search for it. Hopefully, you don't have to travel as far as me.

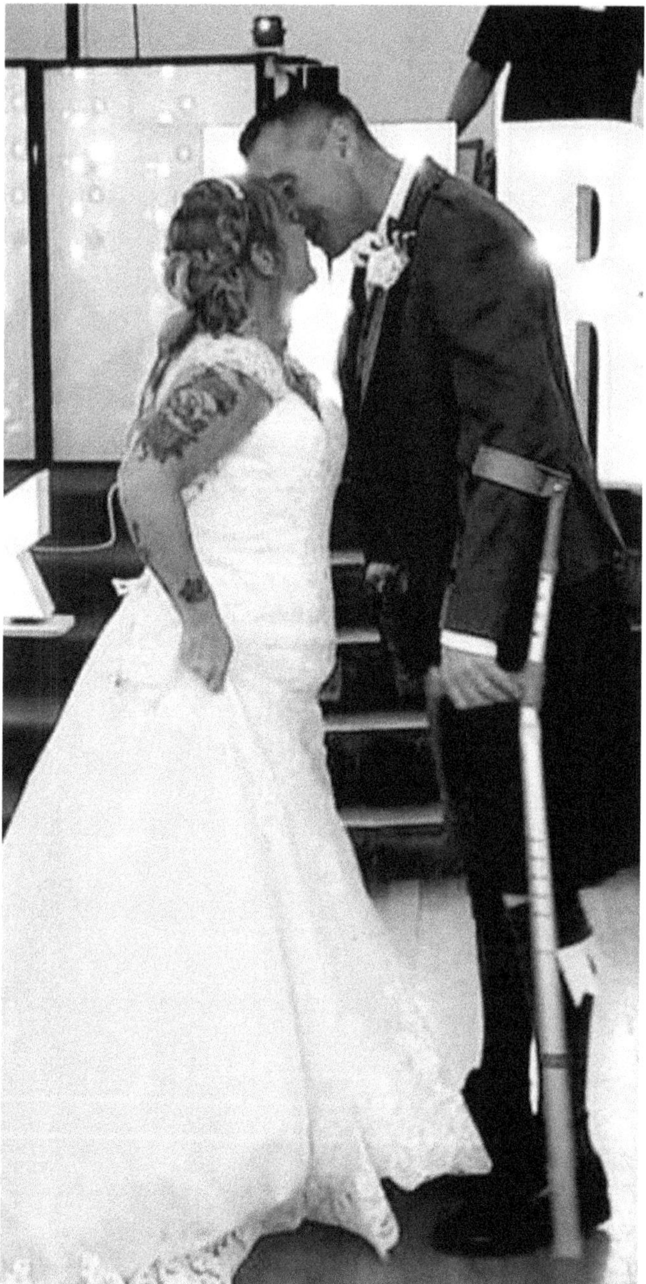

For my freind Franmy
One of the most
Loyal Loving Guys
I Have the great
Pleasure of Having
in my Life, His
Beloved wife
Stephanie was one
of the best aswell.
Through the good
the bad and the
really ugly you
have been a constant
support even to this
day, going through
the worst Times of
His Life today (Turn

Has still the niceness, compassion and Love t has still shown me support, This is not Forgotten My Pal you will never walk alone

godbless

Love You Pal